Dancing the Rounds

An introduction to Rasunah's poetry

Lally Grauer, writing in *Native Poetry in Canada,* said: The richly embroidered imagery of Rasunah's poetry is compelling. Her poems can take surprising turns, such as from the natural world to the other-worldly, as in *Yellow Leaves,* or from Canadian worlds to Indonesian in *Dancing the Rounds* – the title poem of this book.

—

My personal objective is to write poetry with distinctive qualities which might have an appeal which is truly borderless. Many of the poems may be seen as 'responses' to literature (such as *Kinanti* as a response to the *Ozymandias* poem). Some of the shorter poems are simply vignettes or 'statement' poems. Another theme is that of 'voices' or speakers from past or present centuries. Those of earlier times embody the timelessness of archetypes, or possess archetypical elements: *Cup Woman, Isti's Sutra, Hyacinth, I Point the Ways, Kartini* and *Kinanti* are examples. Another theme is the narrative element, either subtle or obvious. Finally, while most of the poems are contemporary in style, those with lines which begin with capitals are intended to be understood as formalized, where the subject tone might be grave, prayerful, eulogistic, or ceremonial.

Rasunah

Dancing the Rounds

Rasunah

www.dreamstairway.co.uk

ISBN 978-1-907091-21-6

First published in the UK by Dreamstairway Books

Copyright © 2011 Rasunah

British Library Cataloguing in Publication Data
A catalogue record for this book is available from the British
Library

Printed and bound in the UK by the MPG Books Group,
Bodmin and King's Lynn

CONTENTS
Arranged in alphabetical order

CONTENTS

continued

DANCING THE ROUNDS

this page & I dance by lamplight in nights
before modern conveniences
I join hands with the ancestors
who jigged & drank
thru log cabin living rooms
in the rugged bays of lakesides
whose tree-scraped skies
were cluttered with the spirits of World Wars
& I join hands with all the brown-eyed children lost
or abused and the families whose spirits
are still being broken by anger & greed

by the shadowy flicker of lamplight
I step gingerly over borders centuries old
& watch the repetitive fall of kingdoms
& the lives of princes & saints unfold;
in fields of revelation unceasing
exquisite orchids grow

as I drive to this valley
ringed with the history of desert survival
loved ones past & present recede,
recede into landscape,
are submerged in memory -
so many leaves under snow

the wake of creation,
is littered with the detritus
of what we are: as under a lens,
still transparencies,

DANCING THE ROUNDS

(or only so many hurled stars) ;
are traced onto the page, fleetingly
until it is folded & yellowed

in the dance of worlds,
the pulse of her blood thru our hearts
enlivens the play of words

in time which sanctifies or existence which typifies
the natural illumination of all things, between particles
of dust which permeate the air we breathe,
between shadows irradiated by lamplight on the screen,
dust, leaves, stars scatter, are folded away

THE KNIGHT OF SWORDS

on this new path of delight
every passing fancy
which escaped you,
I kept safe in the name
of your Holiest campaign.

over long winters your hidden dreams
have been hoarded in my cupboard;
& simple strangers who've stopped
to whet their weary lives, who've drunk
my wine from glasses here
fell stricken with Eternity.

that you were called to me
& I have made you mine,
everything left is an unfolding.
it is courtship, it is pleasure,
it is reason - & we?
our swords crossed
on such paths alone.

everything taken for granted
demands respect. Drink!
your love projected as friendship
is now extended as love. Drink!
I have caught your dreams.

Love me closely like the wick
joins oil and flame.
I have called your name.

THE KNIGHT OF SWORDS

through unconditional acceptance
you master all. Peace in your heart!
through fleeting restlessness
love slips through your fingers
like sand. Be attracted!

Crawling from your knees, Call me!
I am your isolation, your reason,
& your pain. Oh how effortless,
the cold night, & Oh how purifying,
the rain.

HOMES

wooden multi-tiered with balcony & garden
on a breathtaking cliff overhanging a lake,
idyllic everything, even the problems were set
in mildest year round climates,
with just enough seasonal variation
to keep things interesting -
better than Hollywood!

could you live here?

3 islands are yours said the Greek,
A Mercedes Benz said another,
& there was the open-ended expense account
pre-nuptial agreement mine to write,
only a day or two for him per month, if only I'd sign
on the dotted line

could you live here?

people say you don't get used to something different
   but you could...

and she laughed. Streams
trickled down the hills.
I will sing for my supper, she replied.

there are places no one has lived before.
there are only so many places
one can live in a lifetime.
some choose, some count, some wish,
some do not premeditate, some have no time.

HOMES

there are states people have not dreamed
because they live them, they live
what has not been dreamt.

some choose, some count, some wish,
some do not premeditate, some have no time.
it is a fragile
form of culture of which I speak,
so delicate it can only be tasted
on certain occasions.

let me tell you where I am going tomorrow.
When my eyes open, I will know.

could you live here?

KINANTI : A FRAGMENT
(Rebuttal to Ozymandias)

this is the river with tributaries which led to the ocean
overloaded with the silt of civilization
whose surface is glazed over with reflections
of genocide. I flowed through borderless lands
in childhood days; the salt in oceans cleansed my blood
no shores were foreign to me;
under the dazzling suns of history
the cool hands of toiling mothers
shook out their secrets & hung them out to dry

this is the mountain over whose rugged, refreshing terrain
& forests, animals & beings
were swallowed whole by memory
over whose wind-swept heights
the intellect of mankind's genius
was reduced to broken debris.
I rose out of limitless aspiration,
& scoured heaven for a resting place.
Buried deep in my womb
were the inspirations of mankind, borne out of my ears,
where snow sweeps sky,
& where the spirit of the times
spawned the issues of the day.

this is the wasteland upon whose aridity
the foundations of will & force are laid.
Know me as shape-maker,
the instrument which fashions glass from dust that I am;

KINANTI: A FRAGMENT

for the sword of power thrown to earth by passing meteorites
& wrought into the scepters of kings
who wielded them that I am;
know me as creator who traced their outlines
as wind follows sand
& out of which all images are authored,
their comings & goings
delineated as sharply as are oases forded overland,
that I am.

MEMENTO

when you were alive
we knew what to say & do
where we were & why
how to celebrate & cry pure tears

when you were alive
we were on alert
this was our work
within ourselves
& the great training
of appreciation of each other,
if not, a code of benevolent
civility was observed

from you we understood
it was not enough to be good,
to be diligent in correcting ourselves,
but to make others feel comfortable

thru training all day every day
there came knowledge
a way within life
which revealed itself
in the movements of the body,
& body parts

the hands for instance
moved according to their content,
& we became familiar with their weaknesses
& strengths

MEMENTO

when you were alive
our legs were lions or servants or light as air
or intolerant of our urgings, they captured
the feelings of others
as surely as others walked in us
or in our hearts & even so,
we needed to observe our behaviors carefully

now, when
life forces mostly of destructive
or denigrating effects swirl madly
thru our beings as tho there were no yesterday
or tomorrow & we, in the center of the maelstrom
which all beings perceive as life,
not quite wondering where or how we stand
feel isolated

if not for you I suppose, knowing how closely
connected to you we were, today

we would have given up long ago,
would have covered our faces with dust,
so willingly done
when you were alive

your grandson sang
the call to prayer at the corner
of your grave
& his call split this world & the next asunder.
in the moments of that day
there was no ending,

MEMENTO

there were only multitudes
rising, flying, borne aloft
in the wake
of your passage

"we will strip you of your body
& you will die"
was what the angel said

in your departure
an eternal unfolding
is being revealed, the man only a man,
the spirit fashioned of God's Will,

it is still mixing,
ascending & descending
these higher life forces
& their workings

beyond these days
when you were alive...

LETTING GO

empty spaces, from which
to sit unnoticed, quietly to watch or navigate,
eventually to establish identity

once in awhile to speak
never in the company of strangers
there were too many strangers
& one had to be careful
in the land of men

living in the leftover empty spaces
which the eyes of women overlooked
if secure in the home-made trappings
which they wove around their men

as though everyone
might be bought or sold
for a smile, not thinking that a smile
might be all you had...

until briefly we met
and listened to all the war stories
lighting 1001 candles until one by one
each succumbed (one day some time later)

still we grew
in emptiness until the space widened
enough to encompass
the planet, over which
we were meant to move...

LETTING GO

until a deluge came & emptied
a quarter of a million souls
from our shorelines

& now...i have returned
have begun to recall from lives
that are still being lived around me
reasons

no stone can be left unturned,
knowing that what might come to pass
shall also pass away,
that something
within me (in the meantime)
ekes, steals, designs or accepts-

in solitude, a perfection of hopelessness,
a certainty of fragility,
all lack of expectation, a divestment
of illusion, an eternal vacation
from aversion &
lets go of the attraction

to life in this world
to which everything clings

MY GENIUS

"i know what i don't know"
you realize, that's an astounding statement
for one to think to themselves, not to mention
that the answer to that is yards long

"my genius came back" after my mom died,
now that i recall,
it had been gone since the car accident I had,
something like 4 years, 7 months, 25 days ago
no way to explain it, but i felt dimmer,
almost ½ conscious
since then

now i feel the difference between
being aware that the line between consciousness &
unconsciousness always wavers
& being aware
that more is felt unconsciously than consciously
now how can someone know this?

2. there's no real "you"
the "you" is a sum total of all you's
some of them matter sometimes,
all of them don't matter all the time
some of them matter all the time,
all of them don't matter sometimes
these statements may not completely describe
what i'm trying to say, in the same way that
they may not completely describe
what I'm not trying to say.

MY GENIUS

there is a real you, the you that i know
who has passed away, the others are not real
possibly because they have not passed away, because
in another way, I have already passed away,
(which may completely describe
what I'm not trying to say.)

4. my genius is the you
who teaches me something
(who doesn't need to recognize teaching & learning
do not need to be reciprocal)
only the master teacher & the master student
know what this means
they both know when someone fails in teaching
& when someone fails in learning

5. sometimes i wish there was
& sometimes i wish there is
a real "you," but when i say that,
what I really wish is that the real you
still existed in this world.

in this world when you were here
I had a chance to meet the real you
as well as the other you, who wasn't in this world.

the real you who isn't in this world now
reaches me only in whispers
or possibly out of the corner of my eye

MY GENIUS

when I become aware of your presence
you have been sitting in ruku a little to the right of me
just as tho you had always been there
& never had to arrive
& never had been anywhere else
& that it was only me
who hadn't noticed

when my Indonesian grandfather came into my presence
 tho, it was different,
it was as tho he poured into my whole being
from top to toe,
like cool water being poured into the top of my head
& the feeling was instantaneously expansive

6. I know sometimes I have to be a little bit crazy...
meaning, I have to join with the others, the relatives
who come into my company once in awhile, they
are in my room or I am in their home, whatever
it's just what people do...

it's not irritating when they don't
it's just irritating that they arrive later or not at all
when they say they will, because
it makes me feel pinned down to a time & a location

7. she chases after her kids sometimes
I know her bark is worse than her bite

MY GENIUS

I used to take pains
to remind people
that they were human beings
but I don't feel this is my role
anymore

to tell you the truth,
it is harder to take pains
to remind myself,
that I need to be a human being
rather than live too unconsciously
for too long, like most people
do.

8. my genius knows everything that it needs to know
instantaneously, without effort
it knows where what it doesn't know comes from
it knows where it doesn't want to go
it knows how fast it gets bored
it knows when its wasting time
it knows when it's sleeping
it knows how to describe something complex
in 25 words or less, it doesn't suffer
fools gladly, it's not too hard to manage
although it used to be. these days, it has far fewer
sharp edges, not that my genius
doesn't have the capacity
to shred something into tatters at will.

MY GENIUS

my genius always recognizes something useful
& new or original
we're not talking art appreciation here
we're talking an original thought, a thought
not written down, neither heard nor spoken before.

when younger my genius sharpened its teeth
on the range of feelings which people might experience
it closely guarded useful potentialities,
it's seeking was wide-ranging –
until it became saturated with the known world
of knowledge to be had

lately my genius is more concerned with spiritual logic
about which others have written books
take 4 qualities: patience, acceptance, sincerity, courage
in which single face in the whole world are you certain you
have seen them?

one day Bapak asked us
to "feel the sway of the banyan tree"
& to "feel the width of the ocean"
we were meant
 to have hearts as wide & as deep as the ocean

but it's ridiculous really, to know what this means
if it's impossible to feel it.

never believe what anyone says
 if you haven't experienced it yourself
spiritual knowledge works exactly like that…

MY GENIUS

just to take 1 quality, for example
when we speak of patience, if it is a spiritual patience,
upon what basis do we decide that it *is* this kind of patience?
there is patience which one requires raising children,
completing a task, waiting for a process of some kind
to be completed,
patience which "works" or participates in the process
patience which 'witnesses' a process while working within it
patience which children exercise
patience which adults exercise
patience which is based on any 1 of several motivations
patience which is based on *none*
of the above mentioned things.
what then is real patience?

we say that God is Merciful.
this is an emulation of what true patience must be
because we know that God is also Compassionate
& to be compassionate you cannot lack
in giving everything a chance to proceed in it's own fashion,
in accordance with its own nature.

the feeling of true patience is deeply peaceful & complete,
there is nothing lacking in this kind of feeling, you know
when it is part of your life
it pours into your whole being
like refreshing water being poured into a cup.

that is only 1 quality. I have mentioned others.
find them in 1 face, in 1 place.

MY GENIUS

if that place is not within yourself, busy or at rest,
you will never, ever
be able to recognize it anywhere else

& when you find the original source of that place
you will be able to say that if you look for patience
you will not find it; if you don't look for patience
you will not find it…

(& that's only speaking about 1 quality…)

it's not like looking for Godot, either, don't be silly.
why? because the original source of Godot
was the author.

but my genius
is the author of this piece.

THE SWEET QUESTION ABOUT SHADOWS

while listening to an anesthetist
sitting there discussing the kinds of bundles & arches
within neurons in the brain which might be disturbed
(since they can seem to be in 2 places at once)
in a scenario which might interest only paranormalists
who conjectured this might parallel reasons for which
energy might be traced by someone 1000's of miles away

and while watching some laser beams bouncing around
when a neuron was split, one beam being refracted
& the other diverted in another direction

& hearing that statement about how
for every action there's an opposite reaction

his question came back to me

& got me to wondering why
I was still awake, because for half a century
I've been waiting to see when they would invent
my dream machine.

the one that attaches electrodes to the brain
& forms accurate images on a screen
of our organic activities within

so it turned out to be a fact,
(another study concluded)
that subjects might influence
the outcomes of positions
of objects if only

THE SWEET QUESTION ABOUT SHADOWS

to a slightly less than anticipated
measurable degree, or slightly greater
than statistically expected…ah yes, but they couldn't
make them fly as far as the gift you gave me

and butterflies represented, it appears, millennia ago,
the trapped psyche of souls, according to westerners
while according to (some) easterners, they represented
an auspicious visit not yet transpired,
though according to me,
it wasn't butterflies but bumblebees…

all this being partly a reason, of course,
for my explanation about a heightened interest in shadows
which fascinate some before a personal trauma arrives,

or fascinates larger numbers of people collectively
prior to the onset of a catastrophe

"there are many things many people do not understand",
I replied,
(to the sweet question he asked about shadows
which had frightened him)
"but this does not mean there is no explanation.
remember that,
because in a reality comprised mainly of possibilities,
a great difference may be obtained in the difference between
what is perceived as real, and what is real,
as well as who is sitting around thinking it, in a world
where time was all there was to be had…
and the best time there is to be had, which is now."

SO MANY WORDS

so many words
& it's still not sure

your splendor surpasses the width of oceans
& it's still not sure

the people are pure or polluted or struggling or trusting,
misguided or ½-hearted or center of the road
& it's still not sure

the scientists are marrying the artists
& cross-disciplinary subjects are being fertilized
& after all of this intermarriage
it's still not sure

the whole world rotated on its axis
& someone said a little thing
which pointed out the lack of faith
we all had in ourselves
after decades of diligence
& perseverance
& the whole world did not stand still

young men with guns stepped up
onto their pedestals & fired a new round
of messages that echoed the prayers
that were prayed since the dawn of time
& it still wasn't sure

all the children who were lost
or found or sat cross-legged on road sides

SO MANY WORDS

or under tables or in their little bedrooms
who dreamt of saviors who they'd been told
would arrive one day, or who prayed with the purest of lips
which recalled the air fanned by butterflies' wings
were the ones to remind us
we still weren't sure

& we walked down ragged
& treacherous roads
& sang the songs
that we knew best

which each in their own way

was the flowering

of eternity

that all the words
in all the books
could not depict
a hair's breadth
of your blessings
which were there
to be received,
was sure

Creator of the Universes
Man does not find Creator,
but that Creator finds the man,
was sure.

SO MANY WORDS

we who have begun
to kneel
beg to kiss
the hem of the universe

we who have kissed
the hem of the universe,
dumb with wonder
wait upon the life you breathe.

DANCING ON THE SAME SHORE

in the summer equinox she watched them fight
the longest battle ever fought & he treated her
as though she were grist for the mill of his talent
& pretended to himself he had no jealousy
which drove him to & from her

there is that invisible way that she may watch
that whatever transpires, it goes without much ado
even laughter cannot eradicate the sensation,
her life that plaything of the gods

that woman laughing & gesticulating
upon the wooden horse in an alcove
in an alleyway has a way of testifying
to such a tradition, such that she makes
the man laugh & forget himself,
such that she marvels at how little it takes

as we speak of the rules of chaos

which are that whatever is organized
no matter how random, by definition
reorganizes itself & there is only a little
consolation in such a plan

how much more marvelous all devolvement
which takes place despite all efforts
to the contrary

DANCING ON THE SAME SHORE

there is that invisible way that she may testify
to the impenetrability yet impermanence
of the mystic water table which underscores
only a seeming transformation of details

no matter what tumult,
no matter which inconsequential gesture,
something communicates itself out of a grander design
& is reborn

i'm sorry these words do not convey
the effect
of a single raindrop
upon a parched & grassy wind-wrenched plain

or that for some reason
there seems so little chance
to make a full-throated difference
in seasons drowned with song

if it is too late to make such a difference,
one thing:
love until there is nothing left to love
or hate until there is nothing left to hate –
you & I will then have reached
the same shore

BRIAN'S TELEPHONE MESSAGE

yes hello this is brian b___
I am calling you from the IGA & the time is 6:03 25 seconds
& it is sunday august the 16th & this is in the pm
& i was just phoning you because
i was going down to your place but i wasn't too certain if you
were home or not
& then i decided to phone instead, so that's what I'm doing
right now.
but, i can phone you back at 7 o'clock so i will do that
& if you're not there then
then i will try again at 8 o'clock
& if you're not there then
i shall try again at 9 o'clock
& if you're not home by 10, then i shall quit till tomorrow
thank you, megwetch
& i just wanted to tell you that i love you thank you bye, bye
now

DISCERNMENTS

About the slippery line
that divides yes from no –
Doesn't matter most of the time.

Although you might not see it that way,
I found a way to measure compassion there.

About compassion which is measured
or merely affordable,
Dime store civility
doesn't matter most of the time
but that kind which erupts spontaneously –
matters

We say patience makes a human being,
But others
Do the pretending & the posturing.
We know behind our backs,
behind closed doors,
It's a different story.

The place where everything begins,
Somewhere in the heart,
the pulse, or elsewhere
The thing that dawns within,
what becomes conscious
Felt somewhere in the brain,
can try to catch it...

DISCERNMENTS

About acknowledging what is sacred...
The breath is drawn in

We laughed yesterday at how some people
Breathe too loudly, that kind of sensitivity
Can be a form of intolerance

We talked about fascinating things
– parts of the body which gesture or flow,
about how our eyes follow
the arcs of movement
& mysteriously,
a rain dance begins on the inside.

WHAT MY GRANNY SAID

in understanding the suffering of those which one helps
no one can fail to be a human being

if there is something to be afraid of
it is **not to be** a human being

you live in a gone world
I don't have to tell you why
take care of yourselves
was one of her messages

the suffering of others is not worth agonizing about
it is worth contributing something toward

care of others needs to be learned nowadays
save a part of your capacity for -
not the agonizing, but the doing...

"do" through your talents
so that you develop yourself as you develop others

if you have forgotten others, you have forgotten your self,
you have forgotten your soul & your humanity

many are afraid they will not survive the suffering of others
but in fact may draw strength from this kind of fear

live for the day that your contributions may be made
& the day that notice taken by others
of your contributions becomes meaningless to you

on that day you are rich in spirit

NAMELESS
(for Sylvia)

when learning to feel
the weight of existence, yet separate
from fragments of evidence,
a finger curling into sight,
which might grace a nose, a sleeve
in such conflict with the purity of skin,
the eyes might only move from side to side
or the jagged edges of a ribbon
biting at her neck as if to perplex

when learning to walk
She hid behind the door, or in a hallway,
out of sight, until she perched upon her legs
& rose safely, only then
venturing into sight

a very arduous thing for one
who could not sense a foot that stood
upon a hardwood floor, or sudden rump
& was mindful of too much attention,
toe-tips curling like violets in frost

when learning to talk
rolled all the words like black-eyed beans
round the tongue or sides of gums
or back of throat & could not catch them
dispersing only clumps of air manipulated
which fell out in consequence --
salivated pockets of sound

NAMELESS

when learning to learn, all knowledge
already given but how
to put it into practice, without being able
to communicate a request
for tools, I need an instrument like this
for which I have no name, in order
to excise a tiny radio resistor, & can give
no explanation for what I have been
listening to, or this intended operation
enlivened only by the movement
of air through the body into limbs, into cells

when learning to love, only angel's wings
fanning a propulsion through the most uncharted
of territories, in an extension of exhortation
to life, whether another's or hers, no matter,
only, that enraptured form of self-preservation
which attempted a certain disembodied
synchronicity, unsuited to this vale of tears
mostly mis-chanced, or abursting full-breasted
through unexpected chinks of sky

when preparing to die
again no possibility of arrangement
in tandem with the knowledge of others,
hiding until all are out of sight & sound
the overhanging of an eyelid, of secrets,
limbs languid, breath outdrawn, expired,
the mind in a swoon of mysteries,
the silken strains of eternity chafing
against the jagged edges of life

INSPIRATION

breath inside that is virgin
arises within of its own accord,
casts aside your labor
extracts the swelling essence
of the moment & everything
bows down, folds into,
contracts with great pleasure
& holds...

then lets go, is withdrawn
as liberated, rides out
in all directions

eyes open have spent
days seeking. patient eyes
record all who endure,

just as the water in a puddle
on a road which receives
the next imprint

is the subject
of all mankind

(about which certainty
no one needs to ask)

thus upon my arrival
I find you everywhere

INSPIRATORS

those who communicated thoughts
from lonely parsonages, unmarried
who opened their minds
to worlds they would never see,

others blind & bedridden who yet could visit
& paint the exotic in words,

those whose lifetimes were filled with integrity,
revelation or vision, or

those who spoke from dark or horrifying
or mysterious places or eras
of the redeeming & lasting qualities of spirit, or

those who breathed life into personalities long dead
so that they stood before you, their gestures or mannerisms
immaculately & indelibly inscribed

inspired me to think of history, reality & the way things go
of human qualities which signified markers in the sphere
of the imagination
moved me to share what could not be shared

the hand that held the book
or the eyes that traced each line
could not be shared
("the heart is a lonely hunter", said one,
the line capturing a 100 pages)

INSPIRATORS

& once the hand constrained by being
writes words selected over others
& releases them from the mind,
starting & stopping once
between hand & paper

the moment is gone

KARTINI SENDS A CLOUD MESSAGE

Politicians, kings, warriors,
lovers, millionaires, beloved of gods.

I see them & they cannot contain
everything you are or shall be

think what you have gained.

how did i understand?
the mirror of future past
reflects what is there to be read.

you who stand upon
the insignificance of your losses,
Don't cry out when you are called.
that is the way. hear your name.

know who calls.
Cover your face & bow down!

YOU ARE MY SUNSHINE

The women who loved you
And the men who loved you
Are crying sweet tears for you
Tonight, their tears are glistening
Like diamonds in the night
To light the journey, the journey
You are making, it is all we can do

I know you can't take me with you,
Though I'm sure you wouldn't mind,
I never thought you would leave
Before me, never ever thought
You would leave so soon, but I'm sure
You stayed as long as you could.

Just that, I'm sure it was enough.

And if you ask me, do I want
To come with you now, I can only answer
If God Wills, I will follow you wherever,
I will follow you whenever, God Wills

And if they ask me why I feel like this
I will only be able to answer
That I don't know why, there is no why,
And I can find no dress to wear,
No shoes, no veil,
There is nothing in this world
Left to wear for you.

YOU ARE MY SUNSHINE

My light, I see your path of light
Above me arching toward your next destination
I am with you in spirit & you in me
I am surrendered to whatever will be,
Whatever will be.

WALKING ON RUBIES

the ocean progresses with the tides
& fills up river mouths...
what *is*,
for the water which swells the rivers
is so
for the ocean which inundates
what it pleases.

fear of freedom
can not stem the ocean tides

when your path was strewn with rubies,
the shadows of your life obscured
the ones you couldn't see
when I held you up in the sunlight,
the more deeply you searched,
the more light there was to see

in accordance with your own nature
I coursed thru your veins,
when I wrote, it was about you.

the world is man-made, my love
it is not about obeisance
to the boundaries of man

fidelity to truth
is a path strewn with rubies,
is an ocean which fills up river mouths,
is a brilliance which takes on light
where shadows used to be

TRANSPARENCIES

never could stomach
      the solitude of togetherness
the holes people drop into
      because of each other

this is not two voices
it is several
we are contemplating
the 'is' of the 'what'
we are calculating
how deeply
the winter snows
will fall

I dream that we are talking
or I talk so we will dream

silence, my old friend
roars into the room on rollerblades
lights candles, rattles the Venetian blinds,
reveals the transparency
of all doings

the leopard draws back his skin
over its teeth & snarls
as if I didn't know
it was always nearer
than anyone cared
to imagine
swallows hard
& slinks into tomorrow

THE LAST BREAKFAST, SHALL WE DANCE?

She: Now where have you been,
Have you been that choosy? Let me guess . . .

Ah yes, you were looking for virgins
without short hair, girls who would listen
& entertain, & wouldn't be there
when you didn't want them to be.
Ah, I see, how you sidestepped me.

Disappointed, disillusioned, were you?
If not looking for comfort anymore, what?
Ah, a self-sufficient specimen, one that winds
itself up & down, with or without you. No?
What then?

Hmm, of course, the perfect match
in mind, body, soul, & weren't they all
lacking something . . something, something —
Even the perfect ones !

So here we are, you looking like the fallen warrior,
Me showing my age first thing in the morning,,
Speechless, a little wiser
Not bothering to wonder why it took us so long,
Getting on with the day.

He: Except, signorita, what about you?
Weren't the pleasant little boys pleasant enough?

THE LAST BREAKFAST, SHALL WE DANCE?

Did the handsome men lack too much intelligence,
Too preoccupied with ambition, perhaps?
No wonder, dear, you never caught my eye.

Disgusted when they all
ran back to mother, were you,
Found out they didn't have anything better to do?
No knights on white horses who didn't cry
At the sight of their own blood?
Really! What really were you thinking?

Ah yes, those bloodlines, the aquiline noses,
the composed men who held their futures in their hands,
the golden boys with all the unused potential,
which never arrived, did it? Except in the storybooks,
or in the logbooks of impotent men...

So yes, Cinderella, here we sit, the glass slipper gone,
the prince & your younger sister long departed,
with the veils of countless illusions drawn back
& precious little left to surmise, sharing our dearth
of expectations at the breakfast table

shall we dance?

SPIRIT MEMORIES

having secured our shores
they are bathed in that silence
which envelopes all suffering

a sense of sanctity
sharpened thru adversity
& confounded by grace
prevents us from cradling them
in our arms

(they also must be saved
from that place
out of which none return
until the time...)

we who have died,
we who have been consumed
by our own fires & drowned
in benevolent waters
traverse paths lightly

upon which,
stripped of our bodies,
inner selves commune
without words

SIGNATURES

I would not
                incline so lightly
this being would not
                further open out
this freedom would not
                be availed
these hands at work would not
                pause mid-flight
these filaments of memory would not
                be shaken so appropriately -

such subtlety of presence would not
                so effortlessly be acknowledged
                nor your tyranny of justice so easily forgiven
your blade would not
                so quickly have sheared
                the cord connecting me to this world
your eyes would not
                so surely have conveyed
                the periphery of limitless reach

our body would not
                have enfolded uniformly
                thru voluptuous celestial turnings
                thru undiscovered space,
                nor conceived wonder
                of that universe traversed,
                encompassed within our wake

SIGNATURES

I would not
        take up this living
I would not
        lay down this knowing
you would not
        continue this breathing
you would not
        assure this giving

you would not
        be stripped
you would not
        die

without this growing
without this blackbird singing

PASSPORTS TO HEAVEN (For Bapak)

1.
Did you go
to a woman's back door
barefoot & dressed in rags
& ask to see her there?

Yes, I did.

And was she the one
you loved?

Yes, she was.

"I stood at the gate
And called her name."

2.
after Grandfather
bids us goodnight
suddenly again
time quickens

traffic jams the roadways
of the forgiven
& those who still despair

smiles glisten
& most fade
while children light firecrackers
in the haste of night

PASSPORTS TO HEAVEN

3.
it is you who is the dreamer
& we who are the dream

you who is the garden
& the gardener
each of us a single seed planted

the mind empties
plans are suspended

the elders fly to you like moths
youngest cry without reason

in this limbo of your absence
the earth trembles with thirst
in the stillness, the grave opens
& we see more deeply into it
than ever before, into the center
of the earth or of the universe

it seems we are looking everywhere

please lay flowers for us, white & gold
from the next world to this, that we
may be guided by their sweetest of scents

we lay flowers for you here, that someday
we may return to you, Grandfather,
In our heart of hearts.

ON YOUR BEING

soft eyes, who knows what they see
hand on belt loop or snap
or arms folded across chest
legs apart, no leaning, no bend
facing dreams, you, a subject
an object, a fire, midnight

at the end of the road
the breath of walking
clarifies the form
about to take shape.

mind applied, empties of intention
waits patiently . . a listlessness arises,
restless in doing
doing in quietness
streams out from centerground
to the next destination,
overrides a stark insight

sit on the horse,
the spirit takes leave,
the feet find wings
over rough ground,
bleeding, taking leave

in the mist I stand watching
fragments of old songs
flickering on the leaves

OLD DAYS

there in the damp little whitewashed hut with lattices
for small high windows & crawling things in that cellar
which I descended so often with only a lighter' s flame,
what woman dreamt of you

what woman rode in a horse-drawn cart up the hill
to cook unsalted fresh vegetables
in lidless, beaten & charred pots,
dreaming night hours away in candle-lit corners,
sketching walls & chairs in which you might unexpectedly sit,
arrived unannounced from wars which we all fight.

how is it in the dawning of every silence, I find you.

That food cut from the stalk the same day it was bought
with powdery cakes I carried; those nights I heard
the young men joking with guitars across the road
around the waiting game of chess
the anonymous drummer the hour before the cock crowed
& the rushing stream which separated them from me
& gave me starry diamond dreams;

the body freshly bathed & all doors secure
before the approaching chill of night
the woman combing her hair to dry
heard you say, the time
I spent with women was with you

OLD DAYS

that woman you bathed,
no longer struggling against the inevitable,
each of those exquisite moments
caused me to marvel, how no one entered
the spaces (between breaths)
that were occupied completely by you

MOTHER IN ABSENTIA

your speech has changed at night you sleep
with your father
but you are too young
to understand
why someone else feeds you
or as others remonstrate & clothe you
the bars around your sweet heart
press more firmly
a wall against your tears
you are too young to understand
why no one dances
or has time for you
 anymore
but I am not far from you, my child

not far from the peaceful oblivion
of your sleep, the flowers or leaf
that you pick from the stem,
from the breath of warm air
upon your little face
or the curls of your hair
or the large brown eyes
that close around
your dream of me.
I am not far from you, my child

& I hear you say:
mother, please come back to me
don't leave me here so young
what's wrong, mother?

MOTHER IN ABSENTIA

why did you leave your only one
why doesn't anyone
talk about you, mother,
anymore?

LIVING IN THE CHILDREN'S WORLD

let's live in a children's world
& eat spaghetti
or bologna sandwiches
as soon as we're home from school
we'll stay up late sometimes
but we'll get up when we want

we'll sleep
in different beds everynight
or on the floor & we'll leave
half the lights burning
or in the middle of the night
we'll play tag around the house
& take showers
& *someone* will bring us lemonade
& then we'll go back to sleep,
maybe

in the afternoon
we'll cut up oranges
& paper & leave
our clothes where they fall
& *someone* will pick them up
& the birds
will be let out of cages
to cling to the curtains
& we'll find sweets
in surprising places

LIVING IN THE CHILDREN'S WORLD

no-one will wear shoes
& we'll cry suddenly
without warning
when green ants bite us
& we'll ferry spiders
dangling by their strings
to more appropriate places

& when *someone* wants us
to tell them a story
we'll be happy
to imagine something
& when *someone*
asks us to sing,
we'll sing !

FOUND POEM: THE TURNIP

Jean Dominique Bauby. Excerpted from review of The Diving Bell
and the Butterfly *published by Fourth Estate Ltd. (1997)*

these *samizdat* bulletins
report on my life
my progress & my hopes

i thought i would shortly be back
in my Paris stomping grounds
with just a couple of canes
to help me along

that city, that monster
with a hundred mouths
& a 1000 ears had decided
to put me down for the count.

at the Café de Flore, the gossips
were as greedy as vultures
who have just discovered
a disemboweled antelope.

they seemed to think
i belonged on a vegetable stall
instead of the human race

but in a ritual that gives the arrival
of the post the character
of a hushed & holy ceremony,
i carefully read each letter from friends

FOUND POEM: THE TURNIP

one day i hope to fasten all these letters end to end
a ½ mile streamer floating in the wind
a banner to the glory of friendship

it will keep the vultures at bay

i thought i would shortly be back
in my Paris stomping grounds
with just a couple of canes
to help me along

LEMMINGS

perhaps one unfed eye
older than you & shrunk with need
fell hungrily open & was emboldened
by your wretched vulnerability
& made a mindless meal of it

by the same token, I am told
we fail in lonely desperation to escape
the means by which we are consumed,
& hurtle fascinated like lemmings
over the built-in precipice

devoured, just perhaps
by what we race towards

I POINT THE WAYS (After Malinci)

When you pass by my gate
tho you knock at every door
only one door opens.

in my mirror
there is an unveiling
in the unveiling
souls are stripped bare
in magic caverns
lifeblood is transformed

at my table are goblets
of exquisite description
& wooden instruments play music
never heard on earth

on the breasts of women
you meet here
are letters written in gold,
their laughter causes stars
to spin in space

only the most diligent
pass by here
I count few
from among every race,
who surrender all
to journey this way...

I POINT THE WAYS

I am a sign
I point the ways
roads converge & split
I point the ways
The People go down

GALLERY'S GREATEST LOSS

my sweetest flowers
grow in me & I in them
look how they open
the curtains to let in sunshine

has been drawing
endlessly for days
upon days upon
months. he is 7
at the art gallery
unseen
draws at a table
& excited he runs
clutching his drawings
to the room full
of objets d'art
can not imagine
where he may hang them,
stops perplexed & innocent.

the tall strangers stroll
eyes fixed on walls
or others.

eventually
he returns to the little
table behind the partitions
& patiently returns
to his task. he draws
a long fat snake with teeth

GALLERY'S GREATEST LOSS

& all of his drawings
are children's versions of
adult visions,
but far more charming,
far more wondrous,
far more pure.

he has taped
his long red snake
below his bedroom mirror.
& announced that
other new pictures
will surround it.
let us see them
when they appear...

THOSE KIND OF MEN

what kind of men
kill people they know
shamelessly or under orders
& father children
who marry each other
& forgive their fathers
in order to free themselves
from their burdens

what kind of human
stands before you
when you pull the trigger

what kind of men scheme
the deaths of others
in their own names
or in the names of their affiliates
for the sake of status

what kind of father
stands before you
when you rip out his throat

what kind of men
turn blind eyes
to the seeds of destruction sewn
when they force others
to die in the shadows
of the agreements they make
for gain

THOSE KIND OF MEN

what kind of child
stands before you
when you lift the butt of your rifle

what kind of men
kill their mothers
rape their daughters
in order to appease
the demons which haunt them
who haunted their fathers
& hunted their grandmothers
& crippled their brothers
like evil dogs
in anyone's or any reason's name

what kind of people
stand before you
before you crush their skulls

with signatures
that mark you
as those kind of men

ROSITA

AAaaahh, my sweet Rosita, she
is the only, the very only
one for me, when I think of you
Rosita I forget
that I am driving this car -
I think only of you & I &
what it is between us that is
driving this car, ah, the first time
I saw her she was dancing
with all the other women,
but you were the only one
I saw, Rosita, I loved you,
loved you instantly!

...& then the second time
Rosita, you were so lovely
at the auction, seated beside me
your perfume kept rising like mist
into the room of my thoughts -
(I want to marry you! something
in me said) you would notice
& shyly withdraw without saying one word
in the conversation
that admitted you loved me -
I know Rosita, you were waiting
for me, well, I am coming Rosita,
now I am making this journey
just for you

ROSITA

we will see, Rosita, we will see
much, much more of your dancing
since I know you want only
to dance for me & my unborn children
in your eyes, then when I have come
Rosita, we can begin the long dance,
I am sure in every way
you have gestures
that answer all of my gestures -
it goes without saying Rosita,
my sweet Rosita, she
is the only, the very --
--only who is this I see, it is Tita,
that most ravishing Tita who wants
to ride with me awhile,
well I will give her
a ride in my car...

now she is gone, Rosita
I have dropped her off
in a way it's lucky
we are not married yet
if I can still forget
even if only while talking to Tita
you will forgive me if I struggled
to think of you then, Rosita, but then
I think if I only have you
no-one else will ever matter to me
again, Rosita -
Rosita!

PASSAGES

soon I will leave everything
& go where none can follow
& there will not be
much to leave behind

that I know, I will
spread out in all directions
& the higher forms of life
will mix into mine
& disperse all that clings
to one place from within

that journey
or emptying
newly undertaken
will interest me more profoundly
than the emptiness I have known
in this world

I have spoken & I have danced
& this world has disappeared
save perhaps colorful shades
of living, no different in the end
from what met my eyes
when I was turned about
in my father's arms

& through the years there were few
& fewer who opened my heart
& filled it with delight

PASSAGES

having their own ends
first in their sight

till I came to my own twilight
& found a waning interest
(as it happened)
in doing all that I might do

& the roads driven shortened
& the pleasing foods drew further
from my hands & the animals slept
without questions & all of the people
dear to me were caught
fully up in other doings
which (as it happened)
intersected less with my pathtaking

until finally today
(now that everything is almost gone)
& I myself have almost been eclipsed
(who reflects that I was always leaving)
feel grateful for whichever understanding
is conveyed in words with the same carefulness
that higher forces "write" me

does it not strike you as miraculous
that within what construction
you are comprised & unfolded
(as in filaments which meet
in water), you are both so finely
created & so easily sheared away?

PASSAGES

(the more reason
that you feel the ocean
in the day, & feel how much nearer
you are to the stars

2.

the day is grieving
    & it is long with loss
       & someone expresses
          a need to know herself
I listen
    & listen

the day is giving
    & full of unshed tears
       solitude becomes me again

I listen
    & listen to

the day is leaving
    & overshadowed by night
       higher life forces
          shape new thoughts

I listen,
    I die to myself & follow how

PASSAGES

the night listens
      the night listens
        the night listens
          to raindrops
            to raindrops
              filled with living

IN THE NUNNERY

on a full moon night
in the nunnery, all the boarders
dream mystical dreams
gripped by the radiance
of the Great White Nun
in the sky

crazed women can sing
most beautiful melodies
not meant for understanding
mellifluous melodies
wafting over the dome

they contemplate men
in childlike fashion
all of which can be mistaken
for wanton passion
by whatever is not everlasting
in most men, who therefore
cannot ferry
the women hiding
in nunneries very far

on these moonbeamed steeds

Ah freedom, the freedom
of traversing the earth
without ever being required
to touch down;

IN THE NUNNERY

the perfect bliss
of a little girl's smile
& the sanctity granted
in the crescent
of their true love's arms

FRESH POEMS FOR SALE

fresh poems for sale
ragged of edge
pink as baby skins
new on the eye
faint as last breaths
irreversibly blatant,
and blissfully naive

fresh poems for sale
steeped in nowness
irritatingly enigmatic
abstractly diffuse
sentimentally mundane
incorrigibly unpredictable,
insatiably insouciant

fresh poems for sale
offhand state-of-the-art,
madly whimsical,
outrageously readable
simply adorable
anti-memorable
prodigiously quotable
stick pins for your hat

FRESH POEMS FOR SALE

fresh poems for sale
blithely ridiculous
youthfully remarkable
stolidly original
subtly suffused
bon mots vivant

& this one's for nothing
just wait & see what happens to you
when you buy it...

A WOMAN'S JOURNEY EAST

your water made me ugly
your men distorted my dreams
your women stripped the furnishings
from my house. wise men
lowered their gaze
in shameful silence, secretive
about real matters of state

your wise women passed me in the street
&, tainted with the dust
of the marketplace, hesitated
until I was lost, while I
cast pearls at their feet

but one of three,
forever alone in deepest silence
kept turning the next card over.
"Play is hard work," she would say.
Mother, Grandmother, still thinks of me now.

"the only nice thing
is to be good,"
a man thought ill of by many
never dealt the first blow himself,
knew the fire I walked through.

And *Grandfather* laughed when the winds
of the universe blew, gave every piece of dust
a day. Lived quite an extraordinarily
normal life, enveloped us
within his soul

TENDERNESSES

caretaker of your children I am everywhere
you have been, all of your countries
with my right hand I have possessed,
and my words have ensnared your landscapes
in the mercury of liquid things. my breath,
my breasts have cooled your temples; my sunlight
tempted you away when you were keening
at the graveside.

caretaker of your soul I am everywhere
you have been, and drunk with your blood
have raced you to the heavens, hidden
your secrets behind the moon; your gardens
of delight I have tended; your clothing I have
purified with tears and washed with stars.

caretaker of your prayers I have kissed
your feet, and the meanest of your servants
has thrown me the scraps from your table;
for all this, I have dined on infinity and my love
spun by angels has blanketed your solace
with awe. Take me up from the core
of roiled earth - I am ascended; lay me down,
my dreams have descended; and wherever
you touch upon longings that seemed faded,
this sweetness that enriched lifetimes
more precisely than gold
has mastered every emptiness.

PRELUDE ONE

Desire, first quartermaster reaches the crest
of the hill at first light,
unleashes the 4 horses:
Anger, Greed, Patience, Acceptance

They tumble down the hill like demons possessed
Clattering over the broken terrain

Reaching the turbulent river at bottom
The lightning-struck eyes of their enemies
Flicker & redden across the divide:
Anger, Greed, Patience, Acceptance

Their head-long plunge
Churns up the waters, which boil and sear up skin, teeth
muscle, bone

Aspiration, second quartermaster screams
Hideous curses from atop the opposite hillside

They are mixed into the waters
And the waters are you and I,
(All passions in the heart)
Our quartermasters
The stuff of nightmares
These landscapes
Our chimeras,

PRELUDE ONE

Our chimeras
Horizon-lines
Tricks of light
 in the eye

Nightfall,
Both quartermasters sleep,
Envision the spit of wounded & dying,
Specks of dust in silvery columns

Surge through vapors of limitless aspiration,
Nameless riders,
Formless space
Out of time

A gathering
A quickening
A surrendering
Opens yet another way

RICHNESS

hearing the lock turn,
no-one calls. does the
vacant alley below
have a say?

I've disturbed him.
on the other side of the world.
a private argument continues

was it only your mortality
that drove you to this point
about which, I've heard
your prayers were real

were you accepted,
broken, hidden, forgotten
in a mountain village,
simplicity your only audience?

as another gate closes
as for differences in worlds,

you could say I closed an eye
to that golden ring
we held in our hands
in favor of what I knew
(if I were you)

whether taking care
to stay where they were

RICHNESS

or daring to cross all borders
in search of proof of innocence
did everyone stick
to familiar territory
in the end?

having been blown
by the wind, which demands
no passport, bitterness
lies in what has not passed
& wisdom unfolds in the heart
according to what is ordained,
for the homeless or at home

CRUMBS OF HEAVEN

let us pray
for the disheartened
& the poor

let us pray
for those who would join us
    from afar
for those we have caused pain
and for those who lack opportunity
    to improve their lives

let us pray
for those who cry
    for their children
& for the children
    who are unsupported

let us pray
for those who have erred
who have made bad choices
& for those who have envied,
    criticized, gossipped

let us pray
for those who feel weak,
who lack courage, patience,
    sincerity, & acceptance
let us pray
for those who lack confidence,
    capacity, & willingness

CRUMBS OF HEAVEN

& those who would give more love,
        kindness and service to others

let us pray
for those who would share
        their cleverness, expertise,
        & manual labor

let us pray
for those who feel inferior
        & rejected,
        cast down or forgotten
for those who feel lonely,
        abandoned, or afraid
for those who are addicted
        or needy

let us pray
for all those who would strive
for the smallest taste
of heaven

let us pray for all those
who would benefit
from the blessings
we have received

EXPRESSIONS

in quiet the deluge of images
ebbs from sight
the everyday thoughts begin to subside
(only just,) there's the beckoning of other worlds
just under the half-open eyelids,
without reason which neither close,
open, nor glaze over
or perhaps they do

it's true we shall not live forever

& like butterflies unsentimental notions
give pause for reflection; they are chimeras,
they are gossamer filaments, of such stuff
as dreams are made, they dissipate
like spider-spun threads
before an ordinary breeze

the machinery has stopped grinding
the breathing of plants can be heard
the metallic tones of greed & anger
& the burdens of patience have been shed;
veils encircling all you's and I's & them's,
as tangible discomforts not lifted
are of no more consequence

in the moment of all arisings & subsidings

the blood of the heart meets the body at rest,
meets the fingertips and the selection
of surrender, the weapon which unlocks,

EXPRESSIONS

detaches, fastens upon the speechlessness
& silence of the spirit; spirit which comprehends

this, is all that is required

and works at the simple expression of being:
no sisters, no brothers, or peopled urgency in the tome
of the hour - a restless restfulness; the vibrancy of respite
(this 'you', is for you, I think) but I pass on...

all my answers have not been given
nor can be, whether the page caricaturizes me,
a slight imperfection, or I do misrepresent

all that there is, or needs to be

it is no great imposition; the matter of influence left
to the more ambitious creators of self-significance
(I care not that a flag or stone marks any departure
which those to come care to consider or query);

but that it has passed, & that all shall pass
& those ways that pass & that not all ways pass
may purport in this manner of speaking, something of

all that there is,

& that it is riddled with remarkable detail,
that it's course is complex nor plain,
that it in total is fragmented or incomplete,
but that it is you or I or them or

this, is complete.

TURNING

there you are walking inside me, I check
& at first you are younger, then I check again,
& you could be older
& without the weight that you carried here,
you just wore it here
were you the one I loved here
or the one I loved there
now I can say
you were both

who were you that I knew when you were here
that told me a secret,
ah yes, I recognized you...
the child of God, the one
who had no children
came to live here again,
child of the father, who then had no father
this time had a father
was loved here by those who could not glimpse
that reality, so much so,
I never mentioned what it was to anyone

now you are with your original father, still peaceful
now in blue robes
so who was i
that I was here & now you visit this woman
whose mother has passed away, who wonders
who was I that you knew when you were here

TURNING

we shall go back & turn & turn
we may go back to the very beginning
when there were two women, Lilith & i
when there were two brothers, you & cain
who shall we be, then & now, & tomorrow
how shall everything change, again...

SPIRIT BIRD

when a knocking accentuates
words spoken in prayer,
a spirit bird comes to you.
it opens an unexpected door
& makes you wonder
about hidden things

be careful because he carries
your thoughts to me.
(don't misunderstand)
what the spirit bird works in your presence
is you. you become your question,
& your unanswered thoughts grow wings.

those who walk in the forest of my silence,
explore a new country.
take care. steeped in eloquent words
I hear more than the words you use.

in my spirit world
the permission to know me
you seek is mine
& the images which reach me
I return

you go nowhere without my knowledge
there is nothing you may touch
which I may not already touch.

SPIRIT BIRD

I too have seen those nations
piled like columns high in the air,
row upon row, each one engulfing
unwitting passersby

the wonderment you can no longer contain
I shall reclaim.
I shall renew your life

surrender all of these things,
& tho I sit far overland, do not wonder
if, in my prayers, you drop your hands & sleep.

STRIKING GOLD

dug a well deep down the walls
of the everyday things that plague –
the news, what you are or are not
going to do, the money you don't have,
how much you have to pay, & what you
might get, dug a well down those walls

underneath thought we were getting to gold
no sirree, just more black stuff, maybe white
stuff lining the walls this time,
thinking wouldn't it be nice
to have a little spice in the life, & found
you-know-what - deeper down there,
dug a little deeper, found a few

discarded dreams, kinda refreshing
when you think of all the dreams
still being dreamt & here we are
wondering how deep the layers of dreams go...

was explaining to one of the guys,
if you're dead, this is a dream, meaning
this is a dream, but you're not dead if you're
still dreaming

I dreamt of saints, nobility, riches, true love
I thought, but wasn't me
who dreamt them, they dreamt themselves up

STRIKING GOLD

& everyone helped & it was such a torture
to see how many were living out dreams
that hadn't died – surgeons, writers, teachers,
painters, auto mechanics, lovers
& what not

tho there was some truth in all of it, most of it
had to be discarded before they cracked up,
well, some of them did

& somehow there was nothing left
but a few little things
like who they were or what they remembered
at a few specific points or pinnacles,
hmm.

so we were told that the dreams
we dreamt while they all might come true,
in fact there wasn't much left to do, but BE
something very simple (at least,
in my case)

do the things
in front of you in order
to find out who
was doing them . . .

& maybe in the end that's how we struck
a little gold...

EAGLE FEATHER SONG

yesterday two eagle feathers came to me
I am white & I am red
I can sing of those things
no one taught

from the quiet, their voices still reach me

I am not male or female
I am white & red

in the old days in woodlands
running above the ground
brought everything from the past
into the present

when the feathers came to me
I heard the spirits sing again

let others speak of native peoples
yet hear no voices like these
I am white & I am red

when the line of our ancestors
is stretched
the white shears away
like tufts on a thistle
before I sip that power

I am red

EAGLE FEATHER SONG

for no reason the landscape
opens up & reveals
long ago times & rivers of song.

mother sings of the young men
whose hearts sang like birds
in their chests

mother sings of the young women
whose feet were so swift

mother sings of the elders
who brought you this song,
of the history
which brought you here

carry these feathers
for your grandfathers, grandmothers
& all your relations

before these hills & rivers sprang
tell them we knew where to live
& who we were
& how it was
in our woodland homes

tell them you know where to live
& who you are
& how it is
in your eagle homes

THOUGHTS AT LARGE

Thinking is like a river of dreams in retrospect,
We are always waking to what we used to do
In the days when we were drowned in the rush of thinking
Which inundated our point of view
until we eventually gave in

To being carried along by this river
until along the embankment
A small twig caught our attention, to which we clung
& declared, I think this, therefore I am.

Amassing a collection of appealing thoughts,
we grew in scope
until the appearance of the growing thicket reminded us
that just as we may choose one or two thoughts to cling to,
we may be more discriminate, & examine our little collection
more closely, only to discover it no longer represented
who we thought we were, & came to the new conclusion:
"No ideas but in things,"

which meant that the source of
our collection bordered on the void out of which all things
were thought, & it was only our attention
to this myriad of branches
which caused the brain to move.

We, the architects, who had constructed
such pleasing structures, became experienced in the content
which these offshoots from the river of life contained &

THOUGHTS AT LARGE

thus, ever perfectionist & creative, we tore down
& rebuilt & recreated at whim, & manicured the collection
to suit renewed & altered visions of our kingdoms
or our universes.

Eventually, we were bored with all this editing and playing,
& having run out of constructions which pleased us,
once again we took respite in the tabula rasa of thought –
drawing closer to the void
from whence all authored images of ourselves
And life as we perceived it, sprang.
Clearly we were able to determine
The folly of our former pastimes…and came to rest.

How tired we had become of the inefficiency of our
unsuccessful collections,
Which, left untended through alternate
whimsical yet seemingly purposeful
pursuits, brought us no further pleasure.

How tired we became
of even the taste of sweetness or bitterness
which all of this experience
had afforded us. Far better to rest, to rest
Until the spirit moved us.

Better to think nothing than to think merely
For thinking's sake,
or for reasons of excitement or boredom.
Better simply to think when moved to think

THOUGHTS AT LARGE

by our inner selves,
trusting in a finer and higher
Arrangement of the universe and of our lives
than heretofore was in our capacity;

Better to permit the emergence of our latent divinity
whenever possible;
& leave what time was left for others to waste.

Taking solace or comfort
in whatever sanctity this world has yet to afford me,
the rushing river of my youth has widened and deepened,
And somewhere in that depth, i mark the ocean tides
As pulses in harmony with the breathtaking passageways
of this world,
Under-riding the turbulence of overhead storms.

WORDMAKER

I was a vessel
& delirious with intention
in early days, collected them
as foundations stones
strewn before the ever-
receding horizon
I was a reservoir
& they flowed into me,
or rose to the surface
& those aerated by light
lost dross & took on lustre

from silken threads
lying in baskets
wove coats of many colors,
fanciful clouds.
I was a rain maker
whose reverent channelling
of essences echoed songs
of natural elements.
I was a painter,
mixed colors nearest me
by hand, dreamt feeling
onto canvas, hid winter supplies
down bottomless wells
during eons of delight

hoarded every weight & hue
which from time to time
separated out into rainbows,

WORDMAKER

(they had a history
 & so did I)
& worlds were born
in the places that we met . .

a lover, seer or alchemist
awaiting in deepest caverns
of shimmering columns of light
near crucibles, seeking
to change gold into breath
finds only those hands
   which shall transform him
finds only those eyes
   which ferry him
across the burning seas . .

LANDMARKS

things which may confuse the mind once more
tap at the window & tho they are not unfamiliar
the mind recalls the romantic exuberance of prior days
& the soul inclines accordingly

or is it that the wizened soul seeks to please,
in giving pleasure to that ephemeral eye
& in seeking throws a veil upon our actions,
that so blessed we reminisce & delight
along our passageways?

who bows down to who?

were it not that the eye could see
so clearly that in taking leave of this,
its current horizon, to surround & attend closely
to the detail of our universe within a life,
we would be no wiser before all
our deeds were done, so that

the "I" which declares "I know no horizon"
encircles all, & passing a waystation once again,
now calculates the overall distance travelled
& so proclaims:

"ah yes, first here it was I smelled these things
when my heartbeat quickened;

LANDMARKS

& this day that I & my former self first met, I captured
her oblivion to her presence decades hence,
her thoughtless detachment from the world
(in which moments the hunger of all mankind
drowns)

WE are living payment deferred.

whereas, reclaiming this spot, at this same causeway,
baggage worn & ears torn open
with the misery which overcrowds each station,
unbidden agonies now sharply underscore
as certainly as do riverbeds,
the uncharted waterways of heaven

WHO DO YOU LOVE?

who do you love?
do you say, this is forever
& it is true?
do you say, it's not you
& what you do to me
but you & I
& how
you can't separate
the sugar from its sweetness
or the bitterness from its salt
because one is the content of the other?

do you say you would die
for each other if it would do
any good, spirit willing,
or hello & goodbye
with equal ease & difficulty?

who do you love?
do you say you & I
make more than two
& nothing is greater
than two of us
& higher power?

is the trace of the touch
as a knife thru water,
the voice a growing comfort,
the rope from which your lives dangle
held firmly between you?

WHO DO YOU LOVE?

are fruits borne
& thorns plucked out
to mark your passages?

what do you say
to the stars & the night sky
& the caravans & the agelessness
of the one you love
when all is said & done?

do you say,
it's you that I love,
you that I love,
you!

& it is true?

HUMMINGBIRD

I am lying in the belly of the mountains
between two lakes
the other soul I have does all the work
(streaks between pen & paper)

I am lying in the belly of the mountains
between two lakes
between dreaming & waking
between depth & shallowness

I am lying in the belly of the mountains
between two lakes
I can count everyone sleeping soundly,
sisters, brothers, nephews, parents, grandchildren
as I waggle my eyes

I am lying in the belly of the mountains
between two lakes
and those still awake in this town at this hour
are wrestling with each other or their fevers

I am lying in the belly of the mountains
between two lakes
where no multitude of images or sentiments
or thoughts like shrapnel
fragment my brain

I am lying in the belly of the mountains
between two lakes

HUMMINGBIRD

where no solutions that never happen
need to reach higher than the clouds

I am lying in the belly of the mountains
between two lakes
where no friends who don't exist
can wish me into existence

I am lying in the belly of the mountains
between two lakes
where no work plagues me
& no love who isn't there
harangues me

I am lying in the belly of the mountains
between two lakes
where no would-be lover
tugs at my ear

I am lying in the belly of the mountains
between two lakes
where no everyday burdens
or illnesses imagined or real
demand constant attention

I am lying in the belly of the mountains
between two lakes
I don't know why some encourage others -
I suppose to make them feel appreciated
& less lonely, but I don't think it does the trick

HUMMINGBIRD

because there IS NO trick to living
I am lying in the belly of the mountains
between two lakes
where there is only living, there is only now.
if I am neither happy nor sad
or, I err on the side of happiness

I am lying in the belly of the mountains
between two lakes
with nothing to do
& nothing I want to do

I am lying in the belly of the mountains
between two lakes
where the spirit ranges, WAY above the clouds
where tiny hummingbird dreams
uncork the world

TAKING HOLD

as I am drawn into a gentle void
I become aware
that you are part of this process

there are 2 people on this bed
being drawn into some ideas of each other
having to do with a juncture
whose immediate meeting points
are all they have in common.

the contraction is an "and"of some kind
it is a "you and me" & that is all

before & after I have nothing to answer for
before & after I have no-one to answer to

the sensation is that you create a result in me
(that I create a result in you
was not something I was attracted to)

how do you go on knowing
you are only what you do

thinking or feeling sometimes
it has something to do with me
not knowing sometimes
I have something to do with you

VALLEY OF THE BELIEVERS

I'll say it this way:

you know they're going to walk deep
into the forest & dissect it, they're going to bring
microscopes & dirt samples & there'll be seekers
of wine & the bread I broke with you
or anyone. they'll peer between the leaves
& note the smudges, yes, & they'll find the bodies
strewn everywhere, & there'll be a collusion
of confusion & blood & screams,
(some of them mine) & they'll gut the place
of gold & emeralds & desecrate my sacred ground
& they'll water down every element
of purity & quality they find,
except for one thing:

by that time, you'll be able to smell me
in their pores, & I'll have touched upon
the essence in them
of every thing, & in that valley of tears
we shall already have become One.

YOU

You have husbands, wives,
friends, mothers, fathers,
brothers, sisters, possessions,
titles, countries, servants,
strength, wine, love, wealth,
gardens, animals, clothes,
beauty, cleverness, authority,
power, command, weapons,
plans, dreams, missions, etc.

I have other things.

UNFORGETTABLE

I have seen
the fathers
of great men
murdered
& great men's
words continue.

I have seen
so many frightened
who might otherwise think
their own thoughts
& I have understood
that to do so
is to be alone.

alone - indivisible
one   - indivisible
unity - indivisible

a bright star
seen once only
extinguished
still lights, adorns
is unforgettable

understand
who you are
be light once
once be light

JOURNEYMAN

somehow convergences between us
braided themselves together every so often

how might a man or woman
be so enigmatic as not to warrant understanding
(the lights are on or off, aren't they?)
or so lonely as to live only
in completely separate worlds

connected only, & connecting only
with kindred souls, moments upon time.

we have all the details, all the facts,
the sightings, the meaningful conversations
yet there are mysteries which separate all of us
over impassable distances, just as cracks
in the earth do not bridge gaps
between one half of one mountain
range & another

similarly we are equally distant
from our Creator sometimes,
reflections in the world
of differences tug at the needles
of the compasses we use
to find True North.

JOURNEYMAN

futility creeps into the wrinkles of aging faces
whenever a new horizon springs into view
& because each step we take is new,
any connection we might feel enshrouds
what is & what will be,
& new hesitations void of joy
blanket the harbours of love
which encroach upon the coastlines
of our journey.

although only a handful are able
to sense what blessings fall,
I remain appraised
of the wake of your passage -
sunlight sparkling over the ocean

...today another 'you' walks
another continent, driven
beyond the beat of drums & hearts
which conceal deeper pathways being carved
through the jungle.

no one may escape the long journey
we have already taken
or what remains of it
or what draws us inexorably to complete it
& to reach our final destinations.

TIME REMAINING

in the days when
we were young &
liked to play
I took her
on moonlit walks &
sung her songs about
the break of day

until I knew her &
there came a time
when she thought she'd
die for the love
of me or perhaps

she still does

but I am older now &
who knows how much
time that remains
to give my heart
away & to whom?

RETROSPECTIVE

she thinks, "like candy we eat life"
fingers wash over the skin,
sweep along the backbone
spread the muscular flaps
spice the meat, heat it until it sweats

she thinks, in the shadow of Jupiter
our protector, we rolled through limitless space
watched the sport of men & women,
swimming in life -
understands the sentiment
time well spent in delirium,
threads away from eternity

she thinks, galaxies within galaxies
barely traversed, all centers penetrated
far behind suns, withered shells
shed willingly, gone, all influence bled
from the casing which was grown in this world
seeded as a dandelion tuft, blown quickly beyond
sight, like so much mist which evaporated

she thinks, all being which is carried out here
strains against its confinements, toward rest
elsewhere, unknown to this place, & how
at first glance, the end of silence & stillness
began. someone held her who must matter,
who through virtue of such beginnings, fulfills
the requirements of bearer...& the customs of living
donned not like satin perhaps but like patchwork

RETROSPECTIVE

within mysteries upon which we are predicated
within life which unceasingly prays, & works so silently,
about which we are wrapped & which imbue us,
from whose milk we are weaned, if not cruelly torn from
(what, we imagine,) promptings which entice our return. We,
however, like infants barely able to stand or remember
most recent steps taken, she thinks,
search for little cushions
to sit upon, only to please our heart's desire
 for that first awakening
which wrested us from sleep so long ago.

until she is the bearer, & is given glimpses
of how in passing the veils of this world were torn,
& turns endlessly toward doing "all that is doing",
who through virtue of such beginnings
fullfills the requirements of bearer

red as strawberries, short-lived as matches struck,
is perfect in patience & lighter than air
wanders from place to place
& claims no home, knows no boundaries,
fills all words with the tinsel of industry,
& the timbre of ancient songs.

A REMINISCENCE

soft eyes, who knows what they see
hand on belt loop or snap
or arms folded across chest
legs apart, no leaning, no bend
facing squarely toward
dreams, you, a subject
an object, a fire,
midnight

mind applied, empties of intention
patiently waiting, a listlessness arising
moves out from the center
to the next destination,
restless in the doing
doing in the quietness

dreams touch upon
your being from outside

the hair responds, perhaps
the system overloads, shuts down,
a stark insight overrides

sit on the horse,
the spirit takes leave,
the feet find wings
over rough ground,
bleed,
take leave

A REMINISCENCE

eyes which see
what has passed
at the end of the road
the breath of walking
clarifies the form
about to take shape.

hidden in mist I stand watching
fragments of old songs
flickering across leaves

ANGEL OF POSSIBILITIES

" How should you be,
creative soul
who is no part of me?

how might you speak
not daring to show
what makes your life force free?

the law wrests
the blood of your essence
& metes it out in love
you may thus yearn to understand
what you may not otherwise know

you are not hidden oblivious
among stars; the practiced eye
makes obvious your signature
each night

how might you know then,
the path which brought you to this place?

you, son of Kings, are enfolded
in my embrace."

my highest desires are elusive angels
which lead the great chase
& the glittering performance you get is breath-taking.
like chimeras, angels chase out forgetfulness or memory
& lacerate your will, vanishing
& reappearing most unexpectedly.

ANGEL OF POSSIBILITIES

in the heat of intense moments,
the coolness of an angel's breath strikes;
Conversely the hot knives they brandish cut through our
most idyllic thoughts with a universal ruthlessness:

like unbidden peppercorns tasted –
or desperately sought after fountains of revelation
angels are above all,
unpredictable, & below all, the price of a prayer.

WORD MEDICINE

what I have to say about words
is that they are not all for you
but for all of you

they are folded inside your body
as you inhale, they circulate
the entire bloodstream in one breath
and evaporate into the heart
where they are condensed
& you can check
the nature of your heart, breadth & depth

when the sky opens up we can see
shooting stars; the persistent glare of planets
draws as they are drawn into wider orbits
we cannot see, but the inner eye
breathes them in & out & for all time
there is a contraction & an expansion

it is said life was breathed into you & it is a breath
& one breath is a lifetime but we are rarely
so close to the moment or to each other

when the sky opens up there is a play
& a sparkling of lights which dance under the skin.
when the clouds move in, the veins
feel a certain pressure.
mist rises & the eyelids droop
as tho the shadows were lengthening

WORD MEDICINE

as tho it were night the coolness of the air
holds all the mystery

I thought of that hurricane & asked it to blow for me
this is something you cannot feel in the eye of the storm
which, in a word, is becalmed

your body I take & consecrate
move this language thru it,
split it into night & day
into black & white & shades of gray

with flurries of color you complement.
whatever happens, it is a mixture
of more than two of us

perhaps of one undoing & one undone
(as the definition of struggle goes)
or of one inseparable from another

. . . but I have digressed, alluded & understated
the power of language
within you

the process of a grain of wheat
which polishes as it polishes another,
which smoothes out jagged edges
is a purification & a prayer.
"as one", of unity
I have spoken

WHAT COLOR IS YOUR ANGEL, PEOPLE?

what color is your angel, people?
is your angel brown or white or red or black or yellow?
did you meet your angel at a crossroads,
in the depth of night, on your deathbed,
on a boat in the middle of the ocean?

what announced the presence of your angel, people?
was it a trumpet, the crumbling of a mountain,
a lightning strike, an earthquake, a dream?
what did your angel look like, people,
how big were his wings, did he arrive on a moonbeam,
was he carrying a scroll, a tablet, a sceptre, a book?

what was the message your angel brought, people?
did he say you would soon be with child, you would unite
nations, you would build a church
upon a rock, you would convey your message
to all mankind, you would be carried
upwards on a golden ladder, you would wrestle
him through the night, you would surrender everything
to God's instructions?

what was the path you traveled with your angel, people?
was it rocky & muddy & filled with trials,
did it fill you with unshakeable faith & love,
were you witness to a sequence of miracles,
were you thrown into a den of lions, raised by kings,
swallowed whole & spat up by a whale, were you able
to part the waters of truth & untruth, were you able
to purge greed & lust from the world's houses of prayer?

WHAT COLOR IS YOUR ANGEL, PEOPLE?

what angel crossed your path, people,
that eclipsed the sun & the moon & the stars,
& filled you to overflowing, with the radiance of Reality?

BLUEBIRD

can't always pray
in the center of a storm
but bluebird takes
the sting away
I know he's flying
this moment

I am the rainmaker's vessel
that lets in the world
the body can only fill up
but bluebird
takes it all away

he is the rainmaker
the wind & the way

I asked his mother
I asked his grandmother
won't you prepare me
to weather his storm

they couldn't control a thing
where bluebird lights
or when he is on the wing
only grandfather knew

I write when he does not
but bluebird is the writer
of these mysterious things

BLUEBIRD

what bluebird gives or takes
if it is not his
comes from the First creator

i face the golden years
& bluebird is on duty
& there's a golden thread
between me & him

that remembers
the promise of return
that reaches further than this world

of families, comforts,
& things that can't be seen

LANGUAGE IS A MARVELLOUS DANCE

Language is a marvellous dance
Of speech organs behind which
Bodies stand or fall, as we are not
The makers of words
Nor do we possess them at all

VIRTUE IN FULL DRESS

lesser beings, having
no other explanation to impose,
extol Virtue
for Divinity's sake

fruits by others tasted
cannot be known
perfection is reached
through your doing, alone

life is taste, & taste,
being acquired,
is naturally known

Virtue in full dress,
whenever encountered
resides in Godhead
alongside Mystery & Secret

STARWALKING

only when we sing **with** you, full breasted
we are sweet as meadowlarks or youthful dancers
weaving lines and patterns there through fields,

spinning and whirling through air

dreams and visions of thrilling beauty
soften the ugliness and squalor of this world

low-hung fog clinging childishly to hillsides
as day encroaches
softens the crudity of destructive acts committed wantonly

only when we waken and greet you
after the agonies of separation
do we remember the fullness and richness of your love

only when our hearts, bedazzled and filled with love
beat fully and in tune with the richness
of what we have experienced

seeking no object, numb with ecstasy
are we fulfilled and enveloped with the radiance

of stars, & with the kiss of living.

SACRIFICES

I have sat under trees
& spoken to animals
& this with the tongue
or the eyes
or the mind
& they have spoken to me
& rushed out to greet me
as though I had been away
a long time, or shouted
to gain my attention

I have given them their due
I have cut their skins, old & young
& prepared them carefully
whether worn from care unworthy of animals
or torn from the eyes of young children their friends
or herded into market baskets

I have chased them over fields
& called them to me
& they lifted their ears
& sang joyfully with me

I have worn their skins
Close to me & stepped over cobblestones
Worn with spit & oil
& they lie between my feet
& filthy ground

SACRIFICES

they lie between the hair
& the skin of my head
& the tropical sun
& the arctic snow

they have coursed through my blood
& warmed my heart & body
they have been closer to me
than any but my children

closer than all of you
who speak to me
as though you have no memory
or knowledge of the beauty
of these things, who seek
to destroy the way
that each person finds
in favor of your own
self interest, never counting
how many sacrificed
their lives for your sake

& there were those who disdained
the coverings of animals & reptiles
favoring only substitutions
made from chemicals & other pollutants,
pretending these were superior
to the likes
of my body whose breath was defiled

SACRIFICES

with the rancid stink
of so-called progress...

I cut their skins ashamed
For how they were grown
Ashamed for how they were sold
& peeled & stripped of their content
who'd waited so long
to find understanding
in death, in the end of shame

& furtively walked down streets lined
with disapproval for the love
I shared with them, that they
Might salvage a minuscule amount
Of respect for their very existence

Poor beings crowded far
From their natural places,
Shot & skinned, their bodies
Discarded on roadsides
& in rubbish heaps
or burned if not sold
cheaply enough to feed
100 hundred times more
than the few who struggled
decades to savor the taste
of such selflessly-given
sacrifices as these.

PETALS & RAIN

when I see them in the distance
mostly it is the pain

I have thought of speaking out
but mostly it is the pain

the earth is opening up
& there are cracks in it

mostly it is the pain
we run from

till we leap far away
& see how this world looks
outside ourselves, a vast distance
from what we have, desire,
do not have, or from what others have

& see how it looks when we are others
& they are us;

see how the world affects
each one of us for better or worse
or how much of this
is a journey no one shares
& a journey everyone shares

far from where the worlds swirl
& turn upon turnings

PETALS & RAIN

thick with process
& thin with the best of all that we are –

life waits in easily born,
in gracefully worn robes

like a child
life skips down dusty roads
toward experience,
the taste of which
is a petal in the sun
is a raindrop on the tongue
is a sweet sensation,
temporarily loaned…

THE BEST MEDICINE

when dona bellisimo's genuine masterpiece
went tick tock & she woke up
between the lines, the world went running
to her door. She wakes up to heart
beats
& every other thing you can see
below the balconies miraculously
leaves you unscathed: thieves shatter
a window & bleed when they yank out
a stereo, swearing; or just as vocally distressed
some other crowd disperses madly
just as amazingly when gunshots fly overhead
& you are unimpressed

this could be anywhere, but it's not
so let us have this conversation
in a burning world about days
when people cared about the bodies
they left behind & creators knew
to avoid what was mundane
like the plague. dona bellisimo
wakes up to heart
beats
& you don't know what world
is flying by anymore between the scalpel's
edge & the bodies of prophets
whose wounds from stem to stern
were closed in the longest, bloodiest
agonies in the memories of mankind.
shaking her hair she still hears the wind

THE BEST MEDICINE

whistling thru their rattling teeth
in the hollows of her throat each night

this madness which afflicts, this touch
of brilliance which sparks the mind
& hurls your body thru a door,
has sent dona bellisimo's genuine masterpiece
into the ecstasies of oblivion. I can prove it
to you. last seen she hung out back
of a gypsy caravan selling a foul smelling
tonic for unmanageable women
which caused a conflagration
which spread over the world. no one
dared to think what they had drunk
nor asked, but like dona bellisimo read

between the lines

of the arrest of a woman
in long black tresses
whose hysterical laughter
caused a public menace
which could be heard in every marketplace
in the world. her only defense,
it was rumored, was this:
a child who runs thru a field
does not ask why the crickets
who live there sing. She runs,
they sing, the sun's rays uplift us
& I feel no separation
from any heart
beat

MEDICINE WOMAN SONG, 2003

I have burned cedar
for the west,
sage for the prairies,
& sweet grass for the east
I have spoken to our ancestors
& prayed for our descendants
& I have played
my medicine drum
which has joined me once again
with the south,
& with the Creator
of all visions

I have crossed this land
some number of times
& made great circles
round it from the air
& from the sea
& by foot

we are no strangers to you
our keepers
of this land
& all the beings
who live in it

MEDICINE WOMAN SONG, 2003

no matter how dwindled
down in numbers
there are those
who shall rise
from among us
to speak of that

which safeguards
us all, which reminds us
of our humility
& our humanity
in the face
of the Annihilators

LIFE STORY

two children had two toys &,
tossing them around gaily,
one of the children was hit,
& began to cry.

nothing else happened

a bunch of teenagers
rushed into the house
where a bowl of fruit
waited on the table.
since there was more than enough,
everyone ate a piece of fruit.

nothing else happened.

since the workplace
was well organized,
the workflow was healthy,
no livelihoods were lost,
& no one was overtired.
they said they liked to work,
& on that day you could see
they worked well together.

nothing else happened.

LIFE STORY

two people went into a room,
engaged in sexual intercourse
& conceived a child.

that was how it all began.

the 1st time this story was told
everyone understood it. Then,
even though it was unnecessary,
it was given a title
to help everyone remember it.

passed down for generations,
eventually its meaning was lost.
once in a while, however, in its retelling,
someone may be heard to say,

"AAHH ! "

UNNAMED MOMENT

easy
light swaying toward
this breeze
upon my branches
which have been waiting patiently

the breeze
rustles the leaves
& knocks on the doors
of wombs which open

my children are shaken out,
whirl in bits of casing
to the ground I shade below me

my pioneers drifting
further afield, perhaps to places
none of my kind
has ever been

& in the magnetism of the stillness
between the cool arms of earth
& new flown seed

they fall into open embraces
& settle into that life born of stillness

UNNAMED MOMENT

the watcher on the hill
witnessing this unfolding
of reality further understands
the cycle of his journey

evolution and devolution
borne inexplicably & silently
out of the work of creation
proceeds relentlessly

such realization
a mere ad-lib
of the moment

MAGICAL THINGS

when I was youthful I heard stories about love
& how the virtue & sincerity of one person
might bring the impossible to a resolution

I heard stories that if you pray good prayers
they will be answered, but you know I'm so sad
I did not hear from you today.

you would think the ocean of reasons
why men & women hurt one another
would serve to deter lovers
from separating, but into old age,
unto graves, they tear themselves apart

sometimes I think magical things
for instance, that these words
will penetrate your soul
& cause you to respond,
or that by feeling the threads which bind us
you will wake purified & courageous

if what I felt were only human
& supposing that feeling it once were enough
& being pleased by you (before)
was all I needed
there'd be no need for magical things
& I could easily give you up,

but I'm still sad,
I never heard from you today.

FATHER

just a white line
a pool of light
& beyond it, darkness

once a year I traveled
with my father. North, north
to the summer holiday
on a cool night

I sat in the back seat
long, long into the night
& got to know the signs

3 curves coming up
go slow here
bump; talking from behind

happy to be kept awake
& keep awake
he was happy, there was

just a white line
a pool of light
& beyond it, darkness

WHOSE

whose mother has been rolled up
in a worn, forgotten carpet
whose brother is toiling
in the mountains
whose long lost father telephones
on a Sunday perhaps from an even greater distance
whose sister holds ladies teas
on the first Tuesday of the month
whose cousin was found badly bruised
with eye swollen shut on a lawn down the street,
whose nephew spends chilly nights from doorway
to doorway, whose friends know you less well than those
whose blood courses through your veins.

do any of these people mean something
to you?

whose castaways stagger down alleyways
& pound on doors, whose children agonize
nightly in poorly made beds, whose girlfriends
& wives put their hands over their ears
to drown out the sounds of multiple rejections,
whose employees' families curse the day
you made this man another slave to your machinations

TOSSING AROUND

that orchid's other-worldly,
grows fastened onto a certain tree,
blooms only on special nights,
you need to watch for it or you'll miss it
& the other way that orchid weaves its spell
is to inseminate all within reach
with its exotic odor, so drop everything
you're doing, that orchid's there
to be admired, incandescently glowing
near the goldfish pond,
just YOU don't forget what it takes
to care for that orchid
or you'll writhe in pain
with what it is capable of suffering
something about that orchid
I'm still tossing around

that crow he's a black fool,
hanging around, making lots of noise
pushing his crowbeak between your fingers feeding,
but you can bet he'll be the first
to graze on your innards
should you decline in strength, that crow
knows exactly what he's up to
just YOU don't forget what he wants
or he'll be gone
something about that crow
I'm still tossing around

YELLOW LEAVES

yellow leaves announced premature change
earwigs crowded windowsills or fell off countertops
fat flies & then the mosquitoes thinned out drastically
hornets buzzing around the sap of the tree
finally burrowed holes underground as the level of the lake
sank, & with it I began yet another year's hibernation

that week my niece called to announce
she'd survived the birth
if not so lustily as her newborn son
& my children's calls quieted one by one
eventually all the curtains were drawn & with them
dreams of the real you still waiting for me
were dreamt in better worlds
in better worlds where the trees were filled
to bursting with yellow leaves that never fell

CABIN No. 8, BLUE LAKE, B.C.

the two bunks behind are shabbily curtained
(we have our villages)
the window to the left shoots down to the river
& canoes. Proust's Remembrance of Times Past
punctuates the line of sight across the table,
straight out the front door window

on my side she-who-sits-knitting
regards each stitch opening onto the abyss
where mother, others wait for her
in the piercing silence

he wore shorts & his spindly legs
moved with my grandfather's furtiveness
but 23 years later in no. 8, this time

my son burbles behind in the bunk
& outside the door round the camp fire
while my daughter & her friend murmur,
draughts from the abyss
sharpen the knife edge of the mind

CUP WOMAN

the disc of the sun
hides in my womb,
the serpent writhes
under my feet.

I rule the 4 winds
animals in the forest
widen my track,
around my head
starlight glistens

I terrify the waking,
in the center
of their lives they feel
the vibration of my touch

my sight turns in their sockets
my blood courses
through fingers which lift water
to their lips

without they are enclosed,
within I expose the beauty
that they have locked away

in the thickness of night
their deaths are mine,
their power & their decline,
at daybreak their sacrifices
glitter in my hands

CUP WOMAN

this way & that
their souls turn
in my hand
& trees bow down
to hear birds cry
in far off lands.

PHILOSOPHICAL REMAINS

There is only expectation
Aversion & illusion
There is no right or wrong
Ignorance prevails & is finite
Unbounded by the universal
Infinity of possibilities

THREE OBJECTS

one side was male
wizened long beard
the other female
full faced
both with mirror or bowl in hand
formed of the same seated body
face in face
curved long lines robed
jade perfect even atop
carved roughness out of
rock

grotesque
this guardian
majestic
teeth curl round
firebreathing sneerholes with
mane Egyptian waves
& tail
this lion

sheaf rectangular bone
curved at each end
old ivory &
black
stripe down center
enameled red words villages mountains
on either side
one hundred slender teeth

BEAR IN THE HOUSE

something harmonious
is something I should have learned well

colors, feelings can be complementary
but are not necessarily, often
like culture and medicine in the same garden,
the way the branches dialogue,
they are not of one mind
& may never be, or may always be

"so long as something has changed for the better"
who bothers to question what similarities there are,
upon which both might rely.

bear & deer in the same field,
for example, do not act upon each other
in the same way, when the storm breaks

MYSTERY MURDERERS

decided you knew everything
couldn't accept anything
caused someone else pain
projected your sins

threw out your children
communicated badly
or not at all, made blanket
statements, lumped everyone
into the bucket

knew where all the boxes were
could tell everyone what went where
but couldn't say what was
IN the boxes, hmmm

y'all made shrines
of your holiness, your desires,
your marriages, your compassion
y'all made shrines of the attention
due you, & who now will say
he's done someone wrong

y' told me self-interest was just
human nature, & who now
will say he's done someone wrong

MYSTERY MURDERERS

wake up guys, God
is not a True Democrat
if not auto-rule
is a theocrat - is at least
a technocrat, & y'all
are going to cast the 1st stone...

y'all knew what you were doing,
hanging out your opinions
in the shade of the old oak tree

MEMO TO THE DIRECTOR

Who Fell For The Party Line

Patchworking life from its entrails
Daring to conspire creations
Of spurious name, (Or shall I say dilutions
Of modern day soup concentrations)
Any other extra daily body machine dresses to kill.

Having embraced dependence once again,
All claims to wisdom fall upon shifting sand.
From behind skirts or, coveting pieces of gold,
Through self-serving insight hastily placed
Amid the folds of his desires,
& his visions strung on borrowed demands,
He claims to understand
The business he can not have with others.

Yes I see from the fallout
He's returned in defiance,
Having notched his list of credits
on the handle of his mirror
(do go on, with your collection of openings
& exits, & anyway, whose reflections
are left to salvage
In your cluttered roomful of props?

(...Surrender, my friend, just another word
Denoting fears still left to lose...
So let's not talk of love & things,
With so much left to deny.)

MEMO TO THE DIRECTOR

Deeper holes have been dug
Round the Ground, which thereby
May arrogantly be stepped aside -
No doubt the author searching,
Occasionally, as is *fashionable*
Through the remains of other killings,
& crying "Cruelty!" in the shallow streets

Yet if (all signs pointing in the same direction)
Within forgetting there is remembrance -
So I have reminded you, however you read it,
and faced you before your maker,
(That's right, that's what I said,)
& here's to the empty room
in your mirror.

I swear, between we three,
love is wasted along the way.
But do go on, for if my judgement fails me,
I'll take your sins away.

WORDS THAT DO NOT PASS AWAY

I speak
& before the word comes,
I become it

when the arrow flies
& strikes the heart of fire
every objection is utterly consumed

when the arrow flies
& strikes the heart
of earth, she cradles it
in her nest

when the arrow flies
& strikes the heart of air
the missile ricochets

when the arrow flies
& strikes the heart of light
before it reaches its mark
it has already been re-sheathed

when the arrow flies
faster than lightning
we are one, two, three
& one again

I speak
& before the word comes,
I become it

WOLF

good & bad stories
are matters of attraction
life & death tear at the teller,
the teller mimics the details,
the bared fangs of the story

rejoice over the dead

BOYFRIEND

tossed her in the snow & washed her face,
she chasing, laughing

whisked her from the little room, alarm clock
showed her hell in 3 floors of a house:
bikers, boozers, druggies

fled from her, called her from an airport,
made her fall on the floor, weeping

brought her children,
the white wall filling with little doors & illusions

sharpened her mind, she began to think
for herself, never stopped

showed her regularity, dreamlessness, despair
touched her soul, made it bloom,
filled it with the universe, and separation

left her, who needed no-one
conned her in the twilight,
sanctified her body

watched over her, kept her eyes open
knocked softly on her door with stories.

he reminded her of transience,
& how, mysteriously, the wind blows,

pleaded with her over land, over sea,
"Who? Who will come flying with me?"

ASK NO MORE

Who can explain
Why after all these years
Things still go wrong
But other things still go right,

that the birds ask nothing
yet they sing

now that the infirmity
of old age
approaches I have felt fear
that I may become useless
& be unable
to do anything more
for you

but the birds ask nothing
yet they sing

I have seen
That the more things grow
The more things die
& the more strengths wane,
new weaknesses arise

but the birds ask nothing
yet they sing

ASK NO MORE

& I wonder if I'll look
out my window one day
one last time
before I close the curtains,

& ask for nothing,
yet hear the birds sing.

ISTI'S SUTRA

my heart is as open as the sky
who was there to console me?
not even you, who I loved
you were hard-hearted
not even you, would console me

my heart is as open as the sky
I could not be the only one
to console myself, it is full of sadness
you were not there

the power of wisemen & kings
is dust under my feet
"everything is right in any case"
my heart is as open as the sky

BLUE

blue you
pushes through
blue you veins
curled up toes
transparent skin, she's so tired,
so tired, there's a waterfall
down the living room wall
where the child's eyes grow wide
in silence

blue you, blue you over the lake
nothing but shunting billowy trains
over white caps churning up the sea,
blue's what's everything between

blue lake of child's dream
bouncing balls over the rooftops
making it easier, spirit rising from the sickbed
glides easily instead, it's a new game
better not hang around here,
there's a lot more space left, I am swallowed up
in blue

blue lady perched on courtyard wall, suspended
above blue sweet peas sweating blue drops on tabletops
from fingertips on blue stockings in ice-tipped mornings
through the thick tangle of lashes under ice-blue
shadows, clicking the heels

ROLAND'S LAMENT

I put myself in your place & know you. All of your actions
are my actions. I see how in a short few years you are tied
like a dog to pleasing your wife's family.
You gave up yourself for them
& they did not understand what you, my brother, have done.

I myself am exhausted.
Until her family stepped in I was floundering.
I was confused & did not know what to do. Though I hit him
I had to put a restraining order on that man, who tried to tear
my life to shreds, but I have been to court seven times
over this. I knew that I did not understand the language
of the courts. Whatever happens, I will survive,
but with a record
my movements would be even more restricted.

Who shall I be if more limitations are placed
upon what I can do? I am confused sometimes.
I'm not sure if you are who you say you are.
We have just torn out the back wall of our house
& put in a much bigger window. She has done all this.
She has worked all along & I have not put
any money on the table. I am not a viable entity here,
& I have nowhere to go. With my brothers, it is the same.

How shall I speak of vision when I cannot be seen
as I am, when I have created so much of this picture
that others who find themselves part of it add nothing
yet behave as though through their very presence
they are integral parts of it.

ROLAND'S LAMENT

They point to an accomplishment
while I want a machine, a living machine which generates
the spark that propels us into wider forms of discovery.
They have not dreamt these dreams.

My daughter is my daughter & my son is my son.
I have to ensure they do not go wrong, she has felt the sting
of my words. Physically my wife & I are together
in time & place. We are like two trees in the same orchard,
but between us there is no communication. The only answer
I could give her was not enough, but it remains the same:
"Leave me. I am not finished dreaming about you."

TWO MILITARY POEMS

1. FANTASY AT TABLE

i gotta thank that man
i gotta thank that man
for showing me who i am

he was settin up there
in the podium front
you coulda sworn
he was marketing corn
'steada training plans
pre-requisites for some weird kinda
development & I tell you

he had such a BIG mouth
you thought he coulda swallowed
the bombs he was selling
- it was like they was all rolled up
inta a single grain of rice

oh! & there was SO many
intelligent people round that table
why, just this morning one of them said,
if you gotta lose millions somewheres,
you gotta lose millions,
so long as you set that standard.
Set that standard, boys!

some kindsa dreams
got no square inch for peace,

TWO MILITARY POEMS

FANTASY AT TABLE

but i got such a teeny weeny
fantasy: someday I wanna

thank that man
for showin me
who i am

2. NUCLEAR SOUP

mama there's too much soup
we don't wanna THROW it away
what are we gonna do?

what are we gonna do?
what are we gonna do?
we gonna SELL it to you !

any way you want it
we gonna sell it ALL to you !

THE REASON EVERYTHING IS THE WAY IT IS

It is easier to think about something
that you're already thinking
than it is to stop & think about something
that you're not already thinking.

EMAS

Emas the tentative hill I climb trembling
Emas the depth of sickness encroaching
Emas the disparity of dark and light
Emas the dawn yet approaching through my fears

Gold the hollowness of silent night
Gold the reaching out moment
Gold the shaft of moonlit dreams
Gold the day I step upon red soil.

Emas the long winding stair
that mounts the hill I have not yet seen
Emas the leaf encircling pillars
Emas the sunshowers bursting, light years away

Gold the dance of kings and harmonies
Gold the wonder in children's eyes
Gold the pluck of mandolin string
Gold the kettle that calls my company near

Emas the love that's nature's cradle
Emas the hearth of winter's fireplace
Emas the bench carved out of hillsides
Emas the toys in children's flight dropped

Gold the sunflower drooping over fence
Gold the caress in sighs
Gold the garment worn over pure hearts
Gold the unfettered, carefree step

Emas the never-ending breath that enfolds
hands to heaven to earth, & you.

MEMORY SERVES

Were you not clothed by me
Cooked for by me
Did I not sweep your floors?

Were you not cared for by me
Washed by me
Did I not dance for you?

Did I not love you
Desperately, sensibly, freely
Appropriately?

Did I not listen to you,
Follow in your footsteps,
Accept your other wives?

Were you not unkind,
Unaccepting, blind?
Was my blood not equally red?

Did you not ask everything
Of me, and I surrender all,
Unquestioningly?

Loved too much by other men
& women in your family,
Were you not man enough,
To guarantee safe passage
& open up your doors to me?

MEMORY SERVES

Was I not the woman
that sometimes a man needed
and were you not the man
that sometimes a woman needed?
Was my bed not the harbor of your prayers?

Did you not whisper
"True Love is Forever,
You cannot refuse it,"
& did I not accept
that encouragement
in your name?

TINDERBOX DAYS

On one of those tinderbox days
when people get up on the wrong side,
Listen & do ornery, irascible things not for the love
Of their fellows, when they talk a blue streak & don't let you
Get a word in edgewise
 because they are so full of themselves,
There's no room for those of your kind..

On one of those tinderbox days when people can't sit still
& are practically running amok & bristling
with more important things than you have to do,
& they are just so single track
about getting to where they are headed,
you feel the whole world just might burst into flames,
so much so you press that button
to check the news & sure enough, everything you thought
might have gone wrong, is maybe even worse
than you could have imagined,
& if you could have just one split second
to recompose the universe by looking out the window…

on one of those tinderbox days when the sun is fixing to rise
with a vengeance whether you feel prepared for everything
to come on or not,
you seize that little split second
& let it fill
with the tiniest, tiniest whiff of a breeze
from the forest out back,

TINDERBOX DAYS

from the bird sounds & muffled crunching of leaves
depressed or lit upon
by the softest of footfalls & brushings of feathers
& peepings or chirpings in the veins
& the slightest rustle of branches in the crisp, lightening
coolness of the air that has its own manner
of demarcating the outlines of everything that breathes
& radiates serenity in the world around you

on one of those tinderbox days which threatens the sanctity
of the multitude of constructive efforts you have expended
in the quest to redeem
or to salvage the best of what can be expected,
in the face of all that stands the chance of being undone --
drink one long
deep
draft of the secret of life
which bursts from the surface of the pores of divinity,
& which has streamed
from the furthest corners of the universe
to reawaken & unify & purify your senses,
& further fans the vibrations within which are rising
in praise of the gift of life which, miraculously,
you have been given.

TESTAMENT TO GRANDMA

this is what an old man
who drinks & smokes his entire life smells like, grandma
this is what old men
must smell like before they die, grandma,
almost all the same, probably,
this is how they walk when they are old grandma,
I know you wondered about those things,
they were all a mystery,
I know you wished your own mother could have lived
as long as you,
I know you wondered why and how you lived so long,

this is what they do when they are angry, grandma,
they throw fits & talk venomously,
they yank the intravenous tubes out & attempt
to run out the hospital doors, they don't want to die
amongst strangers
they want to be where you are grandma,
smelling of roses,
where your fingers still embroider.

this is what an old man
whose brothers were lost in the war drums like, grandma,
he comes & goes as he pleases
& his children fight against his savagery,
into her old age your daughter loses the memory
of all the painful years,

TESTAMENT TO GRANDMA

she forgets the name of her first-born, grandma
& his only son vanishes before our eyes,
at the bottom of the stairs,
in front of the widow with the widow's chin,
remarrying 2 more men like him who die before their time

his other daughter, nipped in the bud at six months,
you mourned
her sweet watery eyes your whole life, grandma,
with every silken stitch of doll's clothes you made for her -
so many dolls,
 they spilled overtop the upright glass display case,
your grandchildren's fingers eagerly smudged,
swooning over brightly colored ribbons

this is what an old man who spent 75 blustery northern
Canadian winters looks like, grandma,
walking the ties, checking the brakes, with breath like
dragon-smoke frozen over an icy sea of crystals,
face & hands of tanned red leather, unlike the hands of your
own saintly father & mother
arching gracefully round your thin shoulders, holy born

holy born woman I have lived so long your bones have
turned to dust, grandma,
in my dreams I seek the final resting place no one dared to
touch, I watched them run away,
your only one, curious ears straining
heard your body rustle in its shroud one last time
beside the pew,

TESTAMENT TO GRANDMA

even the chubby priest could not linger so long
in your radiance,
the embalmer's eyes, still watering like your lost one's eyes,
lingering with grief over your unimpeachable grace,
drowned in ceremony, aghast
& wandering like a ghost amongst strangers,
your son-in-law's silence a river of testimony
to every steaming glass of tea you ever made,
his shadow today, a testimony
to the indelible fabric you were woven of, grandma

BETWEEN THE RAINDROPS

another child cries, it's 3 a.m. in the downpour
Mom, please let me in! Please!
there is a why, but it has been forgotten

that bird is cold, its head is pulled into its shoulders
& he only looks left & right, waiting for the moment

the great wind god will suck him out into the burly
cloudy-spirit land, i know this because i'm watching
& waiting, too

until the river of blood that brought me to this place
overtakes the mind, the fingertips
until it lies my body down, & fills my eyes
with shooting stars.

THOSE HOT POOR DAYS

those hot, poor days we lived whether overclouded
or bitten & chilled, or in arid indifference we met regularly
& sometimes, looking stealthily to the left & right
of borrowed time as when you drove
a poor woman home to her child

or you facing an old man whose listening
died in your words, an old lady whose words
died in your listening, you trading cubby-holed
meeting places, dressed up or down
shopfronts, roaming through narrow lanes
across parking lots spotted with aboriginal carmine
through scraped stone garrets,
past diagrams, stage models under construction,
phones that worked irregularly, cranky ladies'
& disgruntled men's lives under construction
& coming to terms with your loss of innocence

those hot, poor, undressed days we lived
in fertile hazes, disheveled masks scattered
through the city of rooms & broken trees falling, safeguarded
amorous reliances upon gentle assurances, decry
-ances of shrinking black boxes fallen into
& full of castaways over seas
glittering with human discomfort,
the flight paths of migratory birds

THOSE HOT POOR DAYS

& what a time the people relinquished to light
any of our long nights, real in their strangeness,
strange in their realness, hot with humility,
modestly tracing astonishing hand-to-mouth edges
of landlines fragrantly saturated with human sacrifice,
& the era couched more efflorescently over greatest
distances, where I harvest feathers from the ground.

TANGERINES

Some so thin skinned
They cannot be herded closely together
And are so easily bruised or moulded
That the fruit is easily damaged
And the sweetness quickly dissipated

Some so thick skinned
That the peels take so much nourishment
That no moisture reaches the fruit
& no sweetness can be counted upon
Or remains

Some spray bitterness tartly
When broken open, in direct contrast
To the sweetness within

So that we may say
What the lover is not willing to seek out
The predator will destroy

PISTACHIOS

A little warmth splits a tiny portion
Of the hard shell before it is prepared
For market. Fingernails then open
& release the seed

Too strong, too resilient,
The seed is in danger
Of being opened only with great difficulty...
Or not being opened at all,
Or the shell not being dissolved
Soon after reaching soil

In this way, a few may remain strong
Until the end, without consolation

So that while others may easily say
There is strength in never being opened
For us, there is no strength to be gained
 From never having been born…

MY GENIUS 2

one day I entered my mansion on a mountaintop,
filled with rich brocade
and ran up to my sumptuous bedroom
with huge draping curtains,
bay windows the height of 2 men and the width of 20,
a king-sized poster bed strewn with white satin sheets

only this time,
the palest & most exquisitely beautiful of young men lay in it

I went up to him & it was sure that he was dying,
he was so weakly
he could not walk,
how in God's name, could I make him well?

still strong in age,
I gathered him up in my arms and carried him
toward the bay windows

"Come with me," I said, "I will show you the world"

& there the jewel-encrusted cities lie below, fanning out
toward the most distant of horizons

MOVEMENT OF LIFE

long ago in a tropical paradise along the shores of Sumatera
after an eclipse of the moon,
God moved the undersea floor
and a quarter of a million people drew their last breaths.

a man beloved by many for his care of the people
on the neighbouring island
knew that that this was a sign God had spoken
and that surely more portents were to occur.

meanwhile he called upon one of his loved ones in his soul
to visit him.
she whispered to herself,
"why don't you use the telephone, like normal people?"
he knew this was one of her irritations
& that she could have no idea
that he was going home.

he could have no idea
that curiously she had fallen ill
with a mysterious ailment
which the doctors could not diagnose
but which affected every organ,
her hair, her eyes, her teeth, her limbs.

she could have no knowledge
of the deathbed from which he called,
only a handful of playful days remained
in 'the last days of Pompeii'...

MOVEMENT OF LIFE

in as short a time as the 3 moons that passed,
God moved the undersea floor again
& although not quite as many, nevertheless
hundreds of thousands of souls were lost again.
in that very same hour,
he took her loved one, too.

HYACINTH & BLUE

Another death
Another door
Made of Hyacinth
& blue

About Rasunah

Of Anishinabe/Ojibwe and French heritage, Rasunah Marsden was born in 1949 at Brandon, Manitoba and lived until the age of seventeen on the Canadian Forces Base at nearby Shilo where her father served in the army. Moving to the west coast to attend university, Rasunah received a Bachelor of Arts in English Literature from Simon Fraser University in 1974. She also completed teacher certification and course work for a Masters in Fine Arts in Creative Writing at the University of British Columbia. "Studying with George Woodcock and others at UBC was encouraging" says Rasunah. "They were critical but they enjoyed what they were doing – this was the greatest inspiration."

Rasunah traveled to "discover other states of mind". After a year in Brisbane, Rasunah spent seven years in Jakarta, Indonesia, where she taught English language courses, worked in Telemedia, a tech-transfer company and for Matari Advertising. "I purposefully opened myself to various disciplines of writing–technical, educational, commercial–because I wanted to break the 'post-romantic, neurotic, burnout approach' to what people think writing is; I didn't want to limit myself to a particular literary space." In 1990, she moved back to Australia, where she received a Post Graduate Diploma of Design from the University of Technology in Sydney, Australia in 1993.

Rasunah's says that her travels "have definitely affected my writing in ways impossible to sum up. For instance, people in Java make time for fine attention to detail. They also accept a wide range of human behaviours. Culture is treasured, and lived. Traditionally the kings of Java explored esoteric and mystical practices; they are the cultural caretakers of their people. This was part of their role for centuries."

In Jakarta, Rasunah published a chapbook entitled Voices (1987). In 2000, she received a B.C. Aboriginal Arts Award to compile a collection of her prose writings. Rasunah's writing has otherwise been widely anthologized in *Yellow Medicine Review; Traces in Blood, Bone, and Stone: Contemporary Ojibwe Poetry; Native Poetry in Canada: a Contemporary Anthology; the B.C. Anthology of Poets*, **The West Coast Review,** and *Gatherings*. She also edited *Crisp Blue Edges,* a Canada Council-sponsored, first North American collection of indigenous creative non-fiction.

After living and working in Jakarta, Brisbane and Sydney for fourteen years, she taught creative writing at the En'Owkin International School for Writing in Penticton, B.C. for five years. At the Native Education College and the University of the Fraser Valley, Rasunah worked a further ten years in post secondary Aboriginal education fields as Aboriginal Digital Film coordinator, Associate Dean for Educational Outreach, and Aboriginal Access Coordinator for two campuses and now resides in North Vancouver. She has also been accepted to a second Masters program at UBC which will centre on Aboriginal Research.

Rasunah is a grandmother of three with four grown-up children.